Foh-kus

Jacquie Vo and MM Rothe

Archway Publishing books may be ordered through booksellers or by contacting:

Archway Publishing
1663 Liberty Drive
Bloomington, IN 47403
www.archwaypublishing.com
844-669-3957

Because of the dynamic nature of the Internet, any web addresses or links contained in this book may have changed since publication and may no longer be valid. The views expressed in this work are solely those of the author and do not necessarily reflect the views of the publisher, and the publisher hereby disclaims any responsibility for them.

Any people depicted in stock imagery provided by Getty Images are models, and such images are being used for illustrative purposes only.
Certain stock imagery © Getty Images.

ISBN: 978-1-6657-0723-7 (sc)
ISBN: 978-1-6657-0724-4 (hc)
ISBN: 978-1-6657-0725-1 (e)

Library of Congress Control Number: 2021910314

Print information available on the last page.

Archway Publishing rev. date: 06/10/2021

Beliefs have the power to create and the power to destroy. Human beings have the awesome ability to take any experience of their lives and create a meaning that disempowers them or one that can literally save their lives.

-Tony Robbins

We cannot direct the wind, but we can adjust the sails.

-Dolly Parton

It is our choices...that show what we truly are, far more than our abilities.

-J.K. Rowling

We have, as human beings, a storytelling problem. We're a bit too quick to come up with explanations for things we don't really have an explanation for.

-Malcolm Gladwell

If other people's opinions can shift your "Why", it is not powerful enough.

-*Jamie Kern Lima*

Be thankful for what you have; you'll end up having more. If you concentrate on what you don't have, you will never, ever have enough.

-Oprah Winfrey

You've got to visualize where you're headed and be very clear about it. Take a Polaroid picture of where you're going to be in a few years.

-Sara Blakely

If you have been brutally broken but still have the courage to be gentle to other living beings, then you're a badass with an angel of a heart.

-Keanu Reeves

You think focusing is about saying "Yes." No. Focusing is about saying "No." And when you say "No," you piss off people.

-Steve Jobs

F-E-A-R has two meanings: 'Forget Everything And Run' or 'Face Everything And Rise.' The choice is yours.

-*Zig Ziglar*

You Are One Decision Away from a Completely Different Life.

-Mel Robbins

The only approval you need is your own.

-Amanda Gorman

If you truly love someone, your love sees past their humanness...

-Michael Singer

Watch your actions, they become your habits. Watch your habits, they become your character.

-*Vince Lombardi*

If you can't control your mind, everything and everyone else will.

Where we put our awareness, and for how long, maps our destiny.

-Dr. Joe Dispenza

The struggles along the way are only meant to shape you for your purpose.

-Chadwick Boseman

If you're serious about changing your life, you'll find a way. If you're not, you'll find an excuse.

-Jenn Sincero

I can't think of any better representation of beauty than someone who is unafraid to be herself.

-Emma Stone

To be true to ourselves, we must be true to others.

-United States President Jimmy Carter

Be more concerned with your character than your reputation, because your character is what you really are, while your reputation is merely what others think you are.

-*John Wooden*

You have to remember the value of your individuality - that you have something special and different to offer that nobody else can.

-Jennifer Lopez

To succeed in life, you need three things: a wishbone, a backbone and a funny bone.

-Reba McEntire

In the future there will be no female leaders, there
will just be leaders

-Mary Barra

Either your dwelling and looking backward, or your optimistic and looking forward.

-Dr. Andrew Huberman

Believe in yourself and all that you are. Know that there is something inside you that is greater than any obstacle.

-Christian Larsen

No matter your position, circumstances, or opportunities in life, you always have the freedom of mind to choose how you experience, interpret, and, ultimately, shape your world.

-Brendon Burchard

Leaders have to see past problems for solutions.

-*Marillyn Hewson*

So remember to look up at the stars and not down at your feet. Try to make sense of what you see and hold on to that childlike wonder about what makes the universe exist.

-Stephen Hawking

There are no regrets in life, just lessons.

-Jennifer Aniston

Inside of me there are two dogs. One is mean and evil and the other is good and they fight each other all the time. When asked which one wins I answer, the one I feed the most.

-Sitting Bull

Printed in the United States
by Baker & Taylor Publisher Services